Sisters
In the Bible

Celebrate Relationships
Experience God's Power

Julie-Allyson Ieron

To the Reader

I write to you as a friend—as a fellow journeyer on the trek toward knowing God in new and intimate ways. Like you, I'm busy. I'm often overwhelmed and frequently weary. I don't need one more assignment to add to my long to-do list that would take well into the second Tuesday of next week to complete. And yet, I have a longing to know God—who He is, what He wants from me, what He has planned for me. As part of that longing, I've been getting to know the many women whose stories appear in His Word. In knowing them—how they came to faith, how they lived their lives, how they interacted with the God of the universe—I have come to understand many new truths about the real purpose God had when He created woman. And I have come to understand something about the real purpose God had when He created you and me.

So, I invite you on this journey of discovery. We'll meet women who had families, women who had a message from God, women who felt the hand of God's Son on their lives. We'll also meet women who faced tragic and trying circumstances, women who made some questionable decisions, and women who found God faithful and true to His word. In short, we'll meet sisters in faith who faced the same struggles we face.

This is a practical journey, one that has a great deal of relevance to the lives we live in this day. So, alongside the stories of Bible women, you'll read brief snippets from women of our millennium—women of faith from all walks of life who are demonstrating what it means to put Bible lessons into practice.

You may choose to take this journey alone or as part of a small group or Bible class. If you take it alone, I challenge you to find a trusted friend who can help you process the decisions you'll make along the way—someone who can help hold you accountable before God for the commitments you'll make to living in a closer and deeper relationship with His Son, Jesus Christ.

If you choose to take this journey as part of a regular group meeting, take some time before going to your meeting to read the brief introductory sections, "For Openers" and "Getting to Know Her," as well as the primary Scripture passage for that week's session.

By taking a few moments out of your week to prepare your heart, you'll find a richer and fuller experience all along the way.

So, come on. Let me introduce you to some amazing sisters, women who touched the heart of God.

To the Leader

I hope you're excited about beginning this journey together. The women of the Bible have so much to teach us as women of the twenty-first century. Their homes and conveniences might have looked different, but their challenges were much like ours. They experienced the stress of raising a family, the frustration of dealing with difficult people and out-of-control circumstances, and the strain of making a living and a home. They also desired to know God and better understand what He wanted to do in their lives.

As the leader, you'll have the great privilege of shepherding group members in their discussions and in their commitments. You'll lead them through the study and guide them toward biblical answers to the circumstances of their lives. It is important that you prepare personally for each session both by reading the text and by praying for God to be present and active during the discussion time.

The body of each week's session contains—

For Openers—a contemporary setting to introduce a key theme from the woman's life and to help provide a modern-day angle on it.

Getting to Know Her—an overview of the main Scripture passage that will help put a real face on the Bible woman.

These first two sections should take about one-fourth of your total session time.

The Word Speaks—a time of reading and interacting with the key Scripture.

Where We Come In—a time of putting ourselves in the scene and making it our own.

These sections also contain sidebars—

- What Others Say
- Bible Background
- Did You Know?
- How It Works Today

Reading and discussing the questions in "The Word Speaks" and "Where We Come In" sections, along with the sidebar content, will make up the majority of your discussion.

However, just leaving your study at the theoretical stage is insufficient for real life change, so we've included a response section that you'll lead your group through. This is the pivotal moment of the study, where theory and insights translate into right-where-we-live actions. Try to spend about a quarter of your session time on these sections—

Responding through Prayer—where participants approach God and seek His guidance both individually and as a group. Group support is key, as accountability accompanies life change, and group dynamics come together in a special way as we approach God's throne together.

My Next Step—a practical, personal commitment toward life change for each participant.

Keep It in Mind—a simple, brief Bible verse that serves as a reminder throughout the week of the choices made in the session.

Take the first few moments of your time, beginning with your second session together, to ask how each participant applied the previous week's commitments. Encourage the group to feel free to share successes and struggles in this non-judgmental time. Holding one another accountable in this way will urge participants to follow through on the commitments they make each week.

I encourage you to do this shepherding prayerfully and with the grace and compassion that can flow only from your own personal relationship with Jesus Christ. At times the women of your group may need a listening ear, a compassionate challenge, or an act of kindness. At times you may need the same. But mostly you all will need a safe haven where you can learn together from God's Word, try and fail, and get up to try again. May your group become a place where God's presence is felt and where many women come to know Him in new and fresh ways.

When God does amazing things in your group, let us know about these victories. Let us share in the joy of His work in your life.

Contact us by writing to—

Wesleyan Publishing House
P.O. Box 50434
Indianapolis, IN 46250
Attn: Sisters in Faith

Or e-mail us at wph@wesleyan.org.

More Sisters in Faith Bible Studies

Courageous Women in the Bible
Step Out in Faith—Live Life with Purpose

Transformed Women in the Bible
Explore Real Life Issues—Experience Real Life Change

Contents

Introduction

When God created the original family, way back before recorded history, He had a plan. "It isn't good for man to be alone," He said. So He created woman. He told the couple to be fruitful and multiply and fill the earth. A quick look to your right or left will show you that this command was obeyed. And as children were born to them, there were sons and daughters, brothers and sisters. The Creator arranged creation—even a fallen creation—so that no one had to go through life alone, not even the punished murderer Cain.

Since going through life alone isn't good for anyone, God places each of us in families. They're often far from the ideal—but they provide a place to fit into the fabric of creation, connecting us to the past and pointing us to the future.

Families define us—they give us a name, identity, purpose, and often a challenge. Because of their nearness, they bring to the surface our rough, grating edges. And because of their care for us, they smooth and polish us to reflect more beauty than we ever could alone. More importantly, families live life together. They live the big events: marriages, births, and funerals. And they live the small events of ordinary days.

One of the closest relationships in a family is among siblings—especially among sisters. Nothing is sweeter than when an older sister looks after her younger siblings—keeping them from danger, wiping their runny noses, and interpreting their childish gibberish.

This sisterhood sweetens as the years progress. The next time you're at a funeral, watch the grieving family interact. Observe how sisters hold each other and weep. If it is a funeral where people of faith have gathered, watch the other sisters, too. They may not be related by blood, but they share heritage in God's family. You'll see them hugging and weeping alongside the grieving family, because the ties of sisters in Christ are stronger and sweeter than any connection blood alone could make.

In this Sisters in Faith series, it is apt that we take time to examine the lives of women in the Bible who were, among other roles, sisters—by blood, by marriage, or by faith. These women at times illustrate the best ideal or the worst depths of sisterhood, but in the lives of each of them we can celebrate the ties that bind, that invite us to go along the journey together, and that keep us from ever being truly alone.

1

God Cares About What Matters to Us

Genesis 29:16–17, 22–35; 30:1–2, 22–24

Charm is deceptive, and beauty is fleeting;
but a woman who fears the LORD is to be praised.
Give her the reward she has earned, and let her
works bring her praise at the city gate.

—Proverbs 31:30–31

Discovery

Beauty flows from inner faith not outer appearance.

For Openers

Sometimes biblical customs don't translate well into contemporary life. It's not that their lessons aren't relevant, it's just that we can't get a handle on their peculiar ways. For example, I am living out the worst fears of the first biblical sisters we'll meet: I am single and don't have children. While this wasn't my first choice and I've sometimes felt disappointed in God's plan, my singleness and childlessness is no scourge, no indication of

God's displeasure, as it would have seemed to women of ancient cultures.

Perhaps you, too, have had occasion to be disappointed—or perplexed—by God's plan. If so, you know that at those moments, we must make a choice. We may choose to be jealous of anyone who has what we want. Or, we may grumble and complain and make ourselves a general nuisance. Or, we may take matters into our own hands to do for ourselves what God won't do. Or, at last, we may place our faith in God and choose to live joyfully. It is our choice.

Between them, these sisters tried each of these options within their unique cultural context. Let's discover together how things worked out for them.

Getting to Know Them

Older sister Leah has lived a lifetime in the shadow of the stunning Rachel. Subject to their unscrupulous father, Laban, the two girls have negotiated an uneasy detente (tension)—until Cousin Jacob comes to town. It's not that Leah doesn't have her own charm— she has striking eyes. But *everything* about Rachel is attractive; for Jacob it is love at first sight. He agrees to work for their father for seven years to marry Rachel.

When the seven years are up, Laban throws a wedding feast. In the evening it comes time for Jacob to go to his bride's darkened tent, but Laban sends him to Leah. Jacob sleeps with her and doesn't discover he has been tricked until morning. He confronts Laban and demands his rightful bride. The father says it would be a cultural taboo for the younger daughter to marry before the elder and unveils his plan to marry the second daughter to Jacob—for seven more years of indentured servitude.

From here things get complicated. Jacob loves Rachel but despises Leah. Leah, though, finds favor with God and begins bearing Jacob one son after another. Rachel has none. Leah hopes after each child to earn her husband's love but is perpetually disappointed. By the time her fourth son is born, she accepts her lot and chooses to praise the Lord. That fourth son she names Judah, meaning "praised."

In irrational fury, Rachel demands that Jacob give her a son. When she remains barren, she gives her maid to Jacob; the maid bears two sons. Not to be outdone, Leah gives Jacob *her* maid; two more sons are born. Finally, Rachel bears Joseph. Even then, she isn't satisfied.

The Word Speaks

Get to know the sisters by reading **Genesis 29:16-17**.

From what you see in these verses, describe both sisters. Discuss their physical traits and anything you can discern about their character. (Note: An alternate translation for verse 17 is that Leah had "delicate" eyes—possibly indicating beauty rather than weakness.)

Now, read verses **22-30**. We aren't privy to the motivations of each character. For example, we don't know whether Leah went willingly or just obediently into the marriage. We don't know whether Rachel loved Jacob. What difference would it make to know some of those details? Why do you suppose the writer left them out?

Did You Know?

The marriage feast . . . lasted seven days . . . and probably Laban wished to keep his fraud from the public eye; therefore he informs Jacob that if he will fulfill the marriage week for Leah, he will give him Rachel at the end of it, on condition of his serving seven other years.

—Adam Clarke

Read the quote from Adam Clarke. Why does Jacob agree to this dubious arrangement? Where is God when this deception is going on? Recall everything you can about Jacob's early life (turn to Genesis 27–28 for clues); how does the deceiver become the deceived? Why is this an important lesson for Jacob? for the sisters?

The trick of pretending He was Esau to steal his father's blessing

Read **Genesis 29:31–30:2, 22-24**. Then scan chapter 30. Despite your cultural distance, allow yourself to experience the escalating competition between the sisters. How much is attributable to their circumstances? How much to their choices?

At what point does the Lord become observably involved? Why?

Is it fair that Leah gets to bear the children, while Rachel gets their husband's love? Why or why not? Why is neither sister satisfied? Why does each crave what she doesn't have?

Read the first quote from S. P. and L. Richards. Why do you suppose Rachel appeals to Jacob but not to God? Note Rachel's action in 31:19, when she steals her father's household idols. What does this scene suggest about the verity of Rachel's faith?

> ### What Others Say
>
> We are not told that Rachel prayed for a child. Rather she pleaded with Jacob. This may well indicate that Rachel in her love looked to Jacob to provide a satisfaction that only God could provide.
>
> —S. P. and L. Richards

Scan the words the sisters say as they name each child (29:33–35; 30:6–7). What do these names indicate about their hearts? What do you make of the way Judah is named? What is changed in Leah? Look at verse 24. What indication do you have that Rachel is bitter despite her beauty, her infant son, and her husband's love? 1) Reuben 3) Levi 4) Judah 2) Simeon 5) Issachar 6) Zebulon 5 seeking acceptance of Jacob 35: 16-20

Note Rachel's end (death in bearing her second son, Benjamin). Also note that Jacob asks to be buried next to Leah (Genesis 49:29–31). How do the years change Jacob's perspective on his wives?

Where We Come In

Read Lori Burns's comments. Then look up Proverbs 31:30–31. How might each sister measure up against these definitions of beauty? How do you measure up? What changes would you make?

How It Works Today

Makeup artist Lori Burns talks about beauty:

"When I was a child I loved makeup. I tried different careers, but I came back to doing makeup. I love doing it not just because you're making someone look beautiful, but you're making her feel beautiful. I love seeing her self-esteem rise.

"But if you're not living the right life, it's not going to matter what you do on the outside. You need to be happy on the inside. Christ being at the center of our lives is the basis for that.

"I don't care if you look like a supermodel. Your beauty may fade away. But a woman who fears the Lord, she's the one I say, 'Wow, I want to be like that.'

"Of course, I'm there to sell and make women feel great, but I pray daily, 'Christ, make me an example. I want Your love to shine through me.'"

How does God's favor elevate Leah's self-esteem better than any human favor could? How does Rachel mistake God's correction for rejection? How does this affect her beauty? Could both sisters have experienced God's favor? Did they? Explain.

When have you felt God's favor? What difference did it make? How did it make you look on the outside? on the inside?

Read the "Bible Background" quote. Why do you suppose God chose Leah's son Judah to father the line of King David and eventually Jesus, and another one of Leah's sons, Levi, to father Israel's priestly tribe. What encouragement do you find in the fact that neither the eldest nor the one Jacob favored (Joseph, son of Rachel) was God-chosen to carry the royal seed or serve in His temple? How does this strengthen your resolve?

> ## Bible Background
>
> Leah began her marriage by focusing on what she lacked and being miserable, but she changed her heart and focus to what she had and determined to praise the Lord . . . her faithfulness was rewarded. "The Lion of the tribe of Judah," Jesus the Messiah, came through her offspring Judah and the priesthood through her son Levi.
>
> —*Women's Study Bible*

Read the second Richards quote. How did God use these convoluted events to draw Leah to himself? On what occasions has He used disappointing events to draw you to himself?

> ## What Others Say
>
> While God didn't change Jacob's heart, God did love Leah. He gave her seven children, and in the process God taught her to seek comfort in Him.
>
> —S. P. and L. Richards

When have you been jealous of a sister in Christ? What made you think this was justified? Did the actions you chose to take make the situation better or worse? How?

When have you, like Rachel in Genesis 30:3–8, taken matters into your hands? How did your actions tempt others to follow you into sin? What do you wish you would have done instead?

When you experience rejection from people who should be protecting you, how can choosing to find sufficiency in God provide a real solution? What do you find in Him that no one else could offer?

Responding Through Prayer

Use this as a prayer starter: *God, I've sinned against You by looking longingly at what others have rather than being grateful for the blessings You've given me. Help me to follow Leah's example by replacing complaints with praise.*

My Next Step

When I'm tempted to complain, I will praise God by

Keep It in Mind

Take to heart James's challenge: *"Dear brothers and sisters, whenever trouble comes your way, let it be an opportunity for joy. For when your faith is tested, your endurance has a chance to grow"* (James 1:2–3 NLT).

2

An Awesome Responsibility

Exodus 2:4–8; 15:20–21; Numbers 12:1–15

*Then Miriam the prophetess, Aaron's sister,
took a tambourine in her hand, and all the women
followed her, with tambourines and dancing.*

—Exodus 15:20

Discovery

A leader of her sisters is accountable before God.

For Openers

"Follow the Leader" was one of my favorite childhood games. One child gets the leader's baton; then, what she does, the others do behind her. Her arms wave, theirs wave; she runs, they keep up; she sings, they echo. Then it's someone else's turn to lead—her turn to follow. The trick is knowing your place in each game. Sometimes you lead; other times you follow. This game packs a powerful lesson: No one leads all the time; we serve as leader or follower at the discretion of the person in charge of the game.

Unfortunately when we leave games behind as adults, we are tempted to seize a leader baton that is not ours. I've experienced the temptation to let my leadership in one area entice me to forget that any authority I have is *received* authority, granted and revoked at God's discretion. Perhaps you've been there, too.

The woman we'll meet today tried this power play at great cost. For in usurping authority, her leadership was tarnished and her gift languished. Let's discover her story and avoid her pivotal mistake—while making the most of her life's positive lessons.

Getting to Know Her

When we first encounter Miriam, she is a child watching her infant brother float amid reedy waters in a miniature ark. After the infant Moses is adopted by Pharaoh's daughter, after the little girl arranges for their mother to be his wet nurse, after the boy grows into God's chosen deliverer of His enslaved people, we meet Miriam again, now a mature woman. We see her here as leader of the women among the Israelites escaping Egypt's bondage.

In this moment she shines. Her voice rings out in synchronous harmony with her leader-brother's song. She uses her gifts with gusto, bringing glory to God. She sings, and she dances. It is as if the women become children playing follow the leader. Moses records that *all the women* enthusiastically follow their role model Miriam.

If only her story ended in this blaze of glory. But we see Miriam later in a less flattering light. She has been leading the women as prophetess, under the authority of Moses and their brother, Aaron, the high priest. The leaders are tired and discouraged from wilderness wandering. Exhausted, Moses assigns some leadership duties to elders. Fearing they're losing their standing, Miriam and Aaron pick a fight with Moses over the nationality of his wife, who isn't from God's chosen race. *Hasn't God spoken through* us, *too? Why does Moses think he's so special? He's married to a foreigner!*

Moses doesn't seem to notice, but the complaint doesn't escape God's ear. He exacts a price for this sin. It costs Miriam public disgrace and temporary pain. It costs the people seven days of waiting until her disgrace is completed. Worst of all, it causes God's glory to depart the Tent of Meeting. A high price, indeed.

The Word Speaks

First, let's read about Miriam in childhood, **Exodus 2:4-8**. What elements of her story give clues about Miriam's leadership potential, even at this young age (probably between seven and ten)?

She watched to see what happened when Moses was found + then took action. She had the mind to think ahead

Comment on the significance of God's using a little girl and a pagan princess to save the future leader of His people. What does this reveal about God?

God can + will use anybody for His glory

Next, read about Miriam's leadership of God's women in **Exodus 15:20-21**. By this time Miriam is in her eighties. Yet she expresses unbridled enthusiasm through exuberant music that engulfs her whole body—voice, hands, and feet—echoing the words and tune her brother composed (v. 1). How does this show the best of how families can work together?

Moses led the men + Miriam led the women. They came together to celebrate the victory

Did You Know?

In Bible times, a tambourine or timbrel was associated with merrymaking and processions (Gen. 31:27). Remnants of timbrels with pieces of bronze inserted in the rim have been uncovered by archaeologists. Thus, the instrument could be shaken as well as beaten.

—*Nelson's New Illustrated Bible Dictionary*

Read the quote about ancient tambourines. Knowing this, when you picture this scene, what jumps out at you?

They used instruments to praise the Lord

Read Psalm 149:1–4. How does this parallel the actions of the women in Exodus? Note God's response (v. 4). If this is true in the time of the psalmist, how do you suppose God responds when these women sing His praises?

He takes pleasure

Bible Background

In the early days of Old Testament history a special place seems to be accorded women in musical performance. The prophetess Miriam and Deborah, a prophetess and judge, were among Israel's earliest musicians.

—*Holman Bible Dictionary*

In the quote from the *Holman Bible Dictionary*, note that both Miriam and Deborah (Judges 4–5) were called *prophetess*, because they served as God's representatives. How does this add to your understanding of why other women followed Miriam? What are Miriam's obligations, given the unique way others respond to her?

Miriam led by example
God example
Appointed by God

She was a servant

24

Now turn to **Numbers 12:1-15,** which takes place two years later.
Put yourself in the position of Moses' wife, Zipporah. How might
you feel to be living among strangers and having your husband's
family reject you? Why is Miriam's attitude toward her sister-in-
law especially offensive? How should God's people act toward
outsiders? She behaved in her own flesh
instead of being Godly

Against whom do Miriam and Aaron sin? What emotions might be
motivating them? Why does God expose and root out this sin?
They sinned against God- pride

Read the quote about leprosy.
How does Miriam's role make
God's response necessary? How
does Miriam's sin impact the
congregation's worship?

> ## What Others Say
>
> Leprosy . . . was a devastating
> punishment because the leper
> had to be put out of the camp,
> unable to participate in, much
> less lead, worship.
>
> —S. P. and L. Richards

They did not worship
till she came in to the Camp

Aaron's role as high priest saved him from leprosy. Nevertheless, he
was affected (vv. 10–12) and he confessed his sin. How do his
repentance and Moses' compassion help bring Miriam's restoration?

What message is God sending to the people? What message is He
giving to Aaron and Miriam? What do you learn about sibling
love from this story?

Where We Come In

As we learn from Miriam, let's examine sin, first. Once sin is gone, we'll be free to use our gifts for God's glory. Since the first step is recognizing the sin, describe a time when you've challenged or usurped authority God set up in your life. What sin motivated you? (For example, was it jealousy? dissatisfaction? anger?)

Considering God's response to Miriam, how do you imagine your sin looked to God? How did it affect other people? What consequences did you see personally?

How can you (or did you) make things right with God and with the person you sinned against? How can you avoid responding in the same way in the future?

What Others Say

God expects those He puts in leadership positions to humble themselves and to honor Him. . . . Comparing ourselves to others is dangerous and wrong. We can feel fulfillment in serving where we are.

—S. P. and L. Richards

Read the quote about what God expects of leaders. How can you avoid the temptation of comparing your gifts to others'? How can you increase your feelings of fulfillment as you use your talents for the betterment of His kingdom?

In what areas has God made you a leader? In what areas has He made you a follower? Who may be watching you and following you? What gifts has He given you that can help build up His body?

Read Mark 10:43b–45, and comment on the source and appropriate spirit of leadership.

Read the story of Debbie Criser's worship ministry with her husband, Dennis. What does Debbie's way of approaching ministry and using her gifts for the benefit of God's family challenge you to do? How does it exhibit the best traits you observed earlier in Miriam?

How It Works Today

Debbie Criser has been a church pianist since she was thirteen. The daughter of a pastor, she married music minister Dennis thirty-five years ago, and is the mother of a vocalist daughter and a pastor son. She and Dennis work together to create meaningful weekly worship services for their congregation. A composer and arranger, Debbie loves "the creative process of carrying the text appropriately with the instrumental accompaniment. It's like putting a tool in God's hands to use the music to have an impact on the listener." She encourages musicians in the congregation to "tie their musical gifts with their spiritual gifts"; to help do this, she creates arrangements that showcase their talents.

The couple has been collaborating "with never a hint of competition" (Debbie's words) since before their marriage. "Dennis encourages the very best in me. His vision for music ministry is something we share. He sets the direction, and I respect his godliness in that vision. It is a joy to know what he needs and to be able to help him achieve it," she says.

How will you be a better worshipper and a better example to God's people as a result of observing Miriam's actions—and of knowing how Debbie Criser approaches her gifts?

Responding Through Prayer

Silently express your feelings to God—whether He prompts you to confess sin or thank Him for using your gifts for His glory. After several minutes alone in His presence, join the others in your group by singing a hymn. "The Doxology" (Praise God from Whom All Blessings Flow) would work well.

My Next Step

The sins of Miriam reminded me of this sin in my life: _____.
I confess it now, and I commit to

The example of Miriam leading the women reminded me of the gift of _____ that God has given me. I will use it by

Keep It in Mind

This week, live out Philippians 2:5–6: *"Your attitude should be the same as that of Christ Jesus: Who, being in very nature God, did not consider equality with God something to be grasped."*

3

In Search Of Justice

Numbers 27:1–7; 36:6–12; Joshua 17:3–6

*Commit your way to the Lord; trust in him and he will do
this: He will make your righteousness shine like the dawn,
the justice of your cause like the noonday sun.*

—Psalm 37:5–6

Discovery

Sisters working together can move God's heart.

For Openers

*A*s a teenager in the 1980s, I traveled with a singing group
that used contemporary music to communicate the gospel.
One of the songs in our repertoire came out of Micah 6:8: "He has
showed you, O man, what is good. And what does the LORD
require of you? To act justly and to love mercy and to walk
humbly with your God." The haunting tune of this song reminds
me even yet that we're living in a world in need of justice, mercy,

and humility. *It's not fair* is our frequent refrain as we look at our circumstances and those of the oppressed, tortured, and forgotten.

As we consider the story of five obscure sisters today, this verse seems apt. These girls model for us how to approach God to seek justice, and how to do so with humility—looking to Him for mercy. From examining their courageous, yet measured, actions, we'll gain a fresh perspective on how God would have us confront injustice in our lives and in our world.

Getting to Know Them

The only lives they've ever known have been wandering in the wilderness. Either very young when their parents fled Egypt or born during the wilderness-circling years just outside the land of promise, sisters Mahlah, Noah, Hoglah, Milcah, and Tirzah have seen it all. They've eaten manna from heaven. They've watched as their parents' generation died in the desert as a punishment for unbelief and grumbling. They've watched God live among them as a pillar of fire by night and a cloud by day. They've watched Moses come down from the mountain with tablets written by God's own finger. And now, at last, they sit poised to take possession of the land. Except for one small detail: Since their father, Zelophehad, died and left no son to inherit his portion, there will be no place that will bear his name in the Promised Land.

Presenting a united front, the sisters bring their unique situation to the attention of Moses, whom they know to be both God's representative and a wise judge. Moses carries the issue to God, and God speaks—upholding the justice of the girls' cause and surprising everyone by allotting them an equal inheritance of land alongside their male cousins.

But the uncles begin to wonder, *What happens when these girls marry? What if they marry outside the tribe? We'll be cheated out of tribal lands.* So, they go to Moses. Again, God speaks, this time stipulating that the inheritance requires the girls to marry within their father's extended family. All five agree—none balking or complaining that this would limit their choices.

After the conquest when Joshua finally divides the land, the sisters remind him of their special circumstance. And Joshua fulfills God's revolutionary promise to the daughters of Zelophehad.

The Word Speaks

As someone reads aloud **Numbers 27:1-7, 36:6-12**, and **Joshua 17:3-6**, make a list of all the ways God provides for these young girls. Compare your lists, and draw observations about why God takes special interest in Zelophehad's daughters.

Read the Bible Background quote, looking for insights about the significance of the

Bible Background

To the Hebrew mind, the term "inheritance" had strong spiritual and national associations extending far beyond the family estate. The land of Canaan was regarded as an inheritance from the Lord because God had promised the land to Abraham and his descendants. . . . Both Moses and Joshua were told by the Lord to divide the land of Canaan among the tribes "as an inheritance."

—*Nelson's New Illustrated Bible Commentary*

sisters' request. In our culture, what value do we place on inheritance? How was the land the ancient equivalent of the family's inheritance? In what ways does it mean something even more to these young women?

Why does God make a big deal about who inherits the land? What does the Promised Land symbolize for the people? Read the promise God gave to their ancestor Abraham in Genesis 15:4–7. How is the coming Messiah foreshadowed in the discussion of the land? What significance can you draw from this connection of the seen and unseen worlds?

What Others Say

These daughters of Zelophehad were intelligent, assertive young women. They were not militants; neither were they doormats. . . . Neither did they instigate a negative campaign of complaints. . . . In today's terms, these young women were "pretty awesome," and a credit to themselves and their father.

—S. P. and L. Richards

Read the comments from S. P. and L. Richards. Then discuss the many times adults around the sisters complained and grumbled against God. What did complaining and grumbling cost the previous generation? How was it possible for five sisters to buck that trend? What encouragement does this offer you?

How does their reasoned, grace-filled presentation gain Moses' ear? How are their actions a "credit" to their father? How do their actions align with Psalm 37:5–6?

Consider the quote from Harold Willmington. How does the way God deals with the sisters show they are "heirs together of the grace of life"? If you were in that setting, how might you feel about your status before God after hearing His answer to the sisters? How does that phrase make you feel today?

Did You Know?

The legal question described here vividly demonstrates God's impartiality and concern for womanhood. Unlike the pagan religions, which viewed females as mere slaves and sex objects, God looks upon both men and women as ". . . heirs together of the grace of life" (1 Peter 3:7).

—Harold L. Willmington

The solutions God provides are outside the box yet they perfectly satisfy all involved. When have you carried a need to God and watched Him come up with a creative solution? What do times like these show you about God's concern for the details of your life?

Where We Come In

What might be some of God's purposes for assembling this family in this way? What might He be trying to tell the people of Israel? What might He want to show you all these years later?

Read Jack Hayford's comments about the attitudes of the sisters

What Others Say

All five daughters manifest a balance between a spirit of confrontation and a spirit of cooperation. The former is illustrated by their attack on injustice and the latter by their compliance with the elders' decision (36:2–12) . . . They reveal a contemporary pathway to overcoming inequality while sustaining a godly spirit.

—Jack Hayford

in Numbers 36, as well as their dependence on God as their "Deliverer/Provider." When have you come to a position of utter dependence on God as your "Deliverer/Provider"? When you carried your need to Him, what did God do for you, in you, or through your circumstances?

What would you list as qualities necessary to "sustaining a godly spirit"? How have you seen those play out in your life? Which do you think God wants you to further develop? How will you begin?

It's hard for contemporary women to understand God's stipulation that the sisters marry within the tribe. To us, it might seem an unnecessary limit to their independence. However, the sisters quickly agree—and obey. When has God placed limits on your freedom? How have you responded? What does the sisters' example challenge you to do the next time God acts in this way?

Suppose one of the sisters hadn't stuck with the others. What effect might that have had? How does their unity aid their cause?

Read John 17:20–21. What role does unity among sisters in Christ have today? When have you seen sisters accomplish together more than the sum of what each could do alone?

God told Moses the concern of the young women was *right;* He also declared the uncles' concerns *right.* This word also could be translated *just* or *honest.* What is *justice?* How have you seen God demonstrate justice? When has He called you to defend a just cause? Have you? What opposition have you met?

Read Michelle Rickett's story. How is her taking on of a righteous cause having an impact on women and girls? If you know instances of persecution of women or girls, share these with the group. Brainstorm ways you can make a difference in these women's lives.

How It Works Today

Many in the West are unaware of the persecution and poverty faced by our sisters around the world. But conference speaker Michelle Rickett is working to change that. She has traveled to some of the most oppressive areas on five continents and has brought back stories of how Christian sisters are enduring grave injustice. These became the impetus for her book *Daughters of Hope: Stories of Witness and Courage in the Face of Persecution* and her ministry, Sisters in Service.

Michelle's ministry is having an unforeseen impact on young girls. Pennsylvania teen Stephanie Rodgers explains her middle-school group's study of Michelle's book taught her and twelve others "how to stand up for our faith and learn about the women who really do [stand up for their faith]! We pray for all women [and men] to be blessed for standing up for Jesus Christ!" Stephanie's group now does fundraising and service projects to benefit the persecuted women they're reading about.

Responding Through Prayer

As you pray today, ask for God's protection and compassion on women being unjustly treated across the globe. Ask Him for direction in how you and your spiritual sisters can make a difference. Listen for His answer and be ready to act on it.

My Next Step

Based on what I've learned, I'll work in every challenge and opportunity this week to act justly, show mercy, and walk humbly before God.

I'll do this by

-

-

Keep It in Mind

As you are considering decisions this week, measure your options against this reminder from Psalm 106:3: *"Blessed are they who maintain justice, who constantly do what is right."*

4

The Hard Road To Blessing

Ruth 1:1–7, 11–17; 2:2–12; 4:13–14, 21–22

May you be richly rewarded by the Lord,
the God of Israel, under whose wings
you have come to take refuge.

—Ruth 2:12b

Discovery

Sisters learn the cost and potential of sacrifice.

For Openers

I've often wondered why all-knowing God placed that tree in the center of the garden. You know the one—the *forbidden-fruit* tree. If it weren't for *that* tree, you and I would still be citizens of a garden-perfect world—with no sickness, no poverty, no sin, no general nuisances. Yet the choice to obey or not to obey is intrinsic in who God created us to be—and thus the presence of the tree demonstrated our clear options. Neither automatons nor robots, we are individuals with liberated wills. How much more meaningful it is to serve Him out of choice rather than obligation.

Choice is woven into the fabric of creation—it's been there since "In the beginning. . . ." Every day is a succession of decisions, of choosing to take the path of least resistance or, as poet Robert Frost explained, choose the road "less traveled."

The sisters-in-law we'll encounter today are faced with Frost's fork-in-the-road dilemma. They've learned about their mother-in-law's God, even purport to serve Him in their own land. But when their mentor chooses to return to God's land, their next move will have unforeseen consequences.

Getting to Know Them

You may recall that God placed blessings and curses on the land of promise. If the people serve Him, they will see great privilege in their land "flowing with milk and honey." But if they turn to other gods, they will see famine, defeat, and distress. It takes only one generation to turn their hearts away—and to invoke dire consequences.

As the story opens, the land is suffering from a famine. Unwilling to wait for the Lord's provision, Elimelech (of the tribe of Judah) packs up his wife and sons and moves from Bethlehem to Moab, the land of Lot's descendants. In Moab Elimelech dies, but his sons marry Moabite women. The family (matriarch Naomi, sons Mahlon and Kilion, and daughters-in-law Ruth and Orpah) continues in Moab for a decade until Mahlon and Kilion also die, leaving three childless widows.

News reaches Naomi that God has provided for His people, so she decides to return to Bethlehem. Ruth and Orpah determine to see her safely home, and the three begin their journey. Soon Naomi pleads with the girls to return to their parents' homes, where they can take new husbands from their own people. It takes some convincing, but at last Orpah kisses Naomi and returns to Moab. But Ruth will not be dissuaded. Her service of the living God is not out of convenience or coercion, but a heartfelt choice. Ruth decisively claims Naomi as her family and Naomi's God as her God for life.

Meanwhile, back in the Promised Land, God is preparing the heart of one of His faithful men, Boaz. What happens next is a stunning example of God's providential care for those whose hearts are set on Him.

The Word Speaks

We'll catch the high points of today's sisterhood in three scenes. First read **Ruth 1:1-7, 11-17** aloud. Be especially dramatic when you come to the dialogue.

What factors influence the family's travels to and settlement in Moab?

— There was a famine in the land - God had threatened to bring on them for their sins Lev. 26:19+20

Bethlehem means "House of Bread"

A fruitful land is turned to barreness to correct + restrain the extravagance + wickness of the people

Did You Know?

Moab is [a] rolling plateau . . . well watered by winter rains brought by winds from the Mediterranean. The porous soil holds enough of the moisture for the villagers to grow cereal crops and to find good pasturage for their sheep and goats.

—Holman Bible Dictionary

Read the description of Moab's landscape. Why was this a desirable location, from a human perspective?

Good for growing crops

Commentators believe Elimelech sinned by taking his family outside the Promised Land. Read Deuteronomy 23:3–6. Do you agree? Why or why not?

Yes - He should have stayed with his People + waited on the Lord

What clues does the writer give that Orpah is as kind and sweet as Ruth? What was Naomi's motivation to send both girls back to Moab? How was her judgment clouded?

- Orpah kissed her & wept
- so they could find husbands

What Others Say

It is very proper for friends, when they part, to part with prayer. She sends them home with her blessing. . . . In this blessing she twice mentions the name Jehovah, Israel's God, and the only true God, that she might direct her daughters to look up to him as the only fountain of all good.

—Matthew Henry

Read the quote from Matthew Henry. Comment on Naomi's prayer of blessing on the girls. Her words indicate faith in God, but would a woman exercising faith persuade Orpah to return to her family when it could mean a return to her people's gods? Why or why not?

It was a test - Many have love for Christ but not enough to give up all they have - TOTAL Surrender. They Love Him-yet leave Him. Love other things more. It had to be their own desire

What convinces Orpah to return to Moab? Speculate on why this argument doesn't work on Ruth. *She knew she was going to be inconvienced. Moab was where her father lived + comfort*

Now, read **Ruth 2:2-12**.

What do you learn about Ruth here? How does her conduct help you understand why she caught Boaz's attention? *She was humble + worked along side the people - Great Faith. Her condition was not good. Getting food only by gleaning grain*

Why was Bethlehem abuzz with good reports about Ruth? *She was modest + didn't glean till she asked permission*

Reread verse 12. Then read Leon Morris's comments on it. How does this picture engage your imagination and make you think differently about God?

> ### What Others Say
>
> The imagery is probably that of a tiny bird struggling under the wings of a foster-mother. It gives a vivid picture of trust and security.
>
> —Leon Morris

Skim 2:13—4:12. Summarize the events—paying special attention to evidence of God's providential hand. How does Boaz become part of the answer to his own prayer in 2:12?

Finally, read **Ruth 4:13-14, 21-22**.

Comparing the genealogy in 4:21 with Matthew 1:5, Ruth's second mother-in-law, Rahab, also was notable. Turn to Joshua 6:17–25 to learn about her. What faith does Rahab exhibit? How does she put feet to that faith? How might his mother's influence predispose Boaz toward sensitivity to Ruth and to God's direction?

How does Boaz's redemption of Ruth and Elimelech's land fore-shadow the redemption Jesus offers to every believer in Him?

Where We Come In

Bible Background

The Book of Ruth underscores an overarching theme of the Bible: God desires all to believe in Him, even non-Israelites . . . He had covenanted with Abraham and his descendants in order to bless other nations through the Israelites and draw all nations to himself (Gen. 12:1–3).

—*Nelson's New Illustrated Bible Commentary*

Read the Bible Background quote. How does God bless all nations through the faithfulness of a few sold-out women? How can He bless your nation through you and your group of believers? What can you do to get on board with what He wants to accomplish in your world?

When Ruth chooses to stay with Naomi, she has no idea her descendants will include Israel's Messiah. How might knowing the eternal results of your choices change your actions?

Read Hebrews 11:1, 31 and 12:1–2. Note how God commends those who exhibit faith in Him despite what they see around them. Knowing these faithful followers are cheering you on, how will you choose from among your current options?

Respond to the *Life Application Bible* quote. When have you seen more faith in new converts than old-time believers? Why is this disappointing? How should those who serve Christ for decades respond in crisis? How have you responded?

What Others Say

Israel should have set the standards of high moral living for the other nations. Ironically it was Ruth, a Moabitess, whom God used as an example of genuine spiritual character. This shows just how bleak life had become in Israel during those days.

—*Life Application Bible*

Ruth exudes obedience and trust. She's a true friend to Naomi through tragic days. Now, we see her reward: a loving husband and a baby prophesied to be unusually blessed. When have you seen God work similarly in your life—allowing painful days, but bringing blessings on the other side? Share these experiences to encourage others to keep trusting God.

Read the story of Sondra Brunsting and her Ruth-like commitment to her mother-in-law. What sacrifices did she, her husband, and her daughters make? Why do you suppose she considers the choice not only worthwhile, but ultimately invaluable? When have you made tough choices that paid unexpected dividends?

How It Works Today

Sondra Brunsting is an RN, wife, and mother. When her mother-in-law experienced an aortic aneurysm that should have taken her life (but instead left her unable to live alone), Sondra had a choice: "We wanted Mom comfortable, secure, and surrounded by those she loved. Yet, I had to be realistic." Sondra struggled with the logistics and challenges of taking the dying woman into her home.

"Mom lived in our home for two years. She was dismissed from hospice because she outlived the contract term. Her unchanged aortic aneurysm provided continued concern, though gradually she returned to activities at the senior center and enjoyed seven more years of productive life. She never did understand why we refused to let her drive."

Sondra now considers the choice a no-brainer. She expected to be selflessly serving her mother-in-law; but instead her mother-in-law gave so much back to each member of the family that no one escaped without being transformed and graciously enriched.

Who needs your friendship and care? How can you come alongside that person and be a Ruth to her? How will you respond if she initially tries to dissuade you or push you away?

Responding Through Prayer

Use this as a prayer starter: *God, I see in Ruth and Orpah's story the difference one choice can make. So, I ask for Your direction in my choices and for sincere faith to obey You wholeheartedly.*

My Next Step

I'll seek out someone struggling with depressing circumstances, and I'll walk through the valley of sadness with her by

Keep It in Mind

Like Ruth, determine to heed Joshua's challenge: *"Choose for yourselves this day whom you will serve. . . . But as for me and my household, we will serve the LORD" (Joshua 24:15b).*

5

Vïve La Différence

Luke 10:38–42; John 11:20–33; John 12:1–8

Six days before the Passover, Jesus arrived at Bethany. . . .
Here a dinner was given in Jesus' honor.
Martha served. . . . Then Mary took about a pint of
pure nard, an expensive perfume; she poured it on
Jesus' feet and wiped his feet with her hair.

—John 12:1–3

Discovery

Sisters should celebrate their complementary gifts.

For Openers

What are you known for? Do you sing a mean soprano solo? Do you thrive on keeping the church kitchen organized or the nursery diaper pail emptied? On Saturday evenings do you pour communion juice or study the Sunday school lesson you'll be teaching to the nine-year-old class?

If someone asked you to rank the gifts in your fellowship of
believers on any given worship day, on which would you place
highest value? The preaching? The musicians or vocalists? Are
those more important than the students who drink in the Word of
God? Are they more important than the janitor who changed the
burned-out bulb above the pulpit or the teenager who shoveled
snow so his grandmother's walker wouldn't slip?

As we'll see today in the story of two sisters whom God entrusted
with two very different gifts, no one gift is superior to another—
and no one gift carries a one-size-fits-all guarantee. These women
will remind us that the different talents we've received from God
are worthy of celebration, as long as we use them in a spirit of joy
to serve Christ and His kingdom.

Getting to Know Them

One sister has gotten a bad rap over the years. While Mary—the
sweet, tender-hearted sister who dotes on Jesus' every word and
anoints Him with costly spices—has been lauded, her sister Martha's
name has become synonymous with one who wrongly chooses
activity *for* Christ over listening *to* Him.

When first we meet the pair, Martha is hosting Jesus and His
entourage in her home. She is frustrated that her sister refuses to
care for the guests' physical needs, choosing instead the non-
female posture of student at the Teacher's feet. Jesus allows Mary
to remain and frees Martha from her self-imposed hostess obligations to invite her, too, to sit and listen. While Jesus chides Martha
for being obsessed with "preparations," He isn't demeaning her
gift or ignoring the value of her service. Later, He will return to

Martha's home—to welcome her service and enjoy a delicious repast just before His trial and crucifixion.

Between these scenes, we encounter the sisters sending word to Jesus that their brother, Lazarus, is dying. Expecting Jesus to come or to speak a word from a distance to cure him, they instead watch Lazarus die. Only after they have laid the body behind a gravestone does Jesus come. With Mary, who must be summoned to His side, Jesus simply weeps. But to Martha, who rushes to His side, He makes a startling proclamation about His power over death. She replies with a statement of belief in Him as the Son of God that would put most of His inner circle to shame.

Then with three words, Jesus demonstrates His worthiness of that faith: "Lazarus, come out!"

The Word Speaks

Have someone read **Luke 10:38-42**.

List as many preparations for Martha's houseguests as you can. Consider the fact that the guest list includes Jesus Christ. What special preparations might she want to make to let Him know how much she loves Him? How could Mary have helped? Why doesn't she?

Comment on the choice Martha makes and on the choice Mary makes. Then reread Jesus' words to Martha. What responses do you suppose Jesus was looking for from each of them?

Now read **John 11:20-33** silently.

Why do the sisters send word to Jesus about Lazarus's situation? Why do they word their message to Him in such a familiar way? What request is implied? Why don't they ask directly?

As Jesus remains where He is, what faith struggles do the sisters face? What is Jesus teaching them by His absence?

Although their words are the same, Martha and Mary respond to Jesus' coming differently. How does Jesus validate each sister's needs in His replies?

Bible Background

Jesus . . . identified himself as the Resurrection (v. 25). This is the fifth of seven "I AM" statements made by Jesus in the Book of John (see John 6:35, "I AM the bread of life"; 8:12, "I AM the light of the world"; 10:9, "I AM the door"; 10:11, "I AM the good shepherd"; 14:6, "I AM the way, the truth, and the life"; and 15:5, "I AM the vine"). This momentous revelation was given to Martha.

—Women's Study Bible

Read the quote from the *Women's Study Bible*. What does Jesus' revelation to Martha in this passage say about His understanding of her? How does it demonstrate that she responded favorably to His earlier rebuke?

Read the quote from the *Believer's Bible Commentary.* Why is it significant that she believed first, before seeing results? How does this alter your preconceptions about Martha?

Scan John 11:41–44. Why is it crucial that Jesus demonstrate His power over death at this moment? Now that the sisters know the end of the story, how are they better able to process all that's gone before?

> ## What Others Say
>
> Martha's faith blazed out in noontime splendor. She confessed Jesus to be the Christ, the Son of God, whom the prophets had predicted was to come into the world. And we should notice that she made this confession before Jesus had raised her brother from the dead and not afterwards!
>
> —*Believer's Bible Commentary*

Read **John 12:1-8** aloud. Then read Warren Wiersbe's comment about it.

Answer Wiersbe's questions for yourself and in light of Jesus' choice. Why did Jesus now accept Martha's hospitality? Why did Jesus welcome Lazarus's tacit company? Why did He approve of Mary's extravagant act of worship?

> ## What Others Say
>
> What would your plans be if you knew you had only six days to live? Jesus took time to visit dear friends and fellowship with them. Mary's adoration not only revealed her love, but it brought joy to His heart, exposed Judas's sin, and gave the church an example to follow. Are the places where you go filled with Christ's fragrance because of you (2 Cor. 2:15–16)?
>
> —Warren Wiersbe

Where We Come In

Have you ever had a houseguest? What preparations have you made for that guest? How did you work to make that guest comfortable on his arrival?

Read the quote from Lawrence Richards. Do you agree? Why or why not? How might this be a freeing (rather than a critical) statement to Martha? to Mary? to you?

When have you tried to do *for* God when He wanted you to sit and listen *to* Him? How did you feel when you were *doing?* when you were *listening?*

If you, like Martha, have the gift of hospitality, how does Richards' statement challenge you? How does it affirm you? What does it tell us all about using our gifts to impress others—or even God himself? What does it imply about the reason God gives gifts to His children?

Read 1 Corinthians 12:27—13:1. Why does this list climax in "the love chapter"? What does that tell you about how God intends you to use your gifts?

Read Romans 12:3–8. How does this variety of gifts serve the family? How does it allow unique individuals to work together to accomplish something bigger than themselves?

Read Lin Johnson's story. How was her first church hindering God's work in and through her life? How is God's orchestration evident in choosing her new worship community? When have you seen God shepherd you to a place at a time when your gifts were uniquely needed?

How It Works Today

After realizing the church she was attending didn't allow women to use their spiritual gifts, Lin Johnson thumbed through the Yellow Pages and noticed a listing for a church several of her Bible college students attended. "I went to visit and never left," she recalls.

Lin's visit was an answer to the congregation's prayer. "They had been praying for two years that God would send a person with knowledge of Christian education to set up and administrate a Sunday school. Then, here I come with a degree in Christian education and the gifts of administration and teaching."

Lin has found fulfillment and joy using her gifts there. The congregation's powerful Bible teaching and friendly fellowship confirmed that she was faithful to God's direction in seeking and finding this place of worship and service.

What are your responsibilities related to the gifts and talents God has given you? In what specific ways would God have you use your gifts for the benefit of His family and himself?

Responding Through Prayer

Have each group member begin your prayer time with words like these: *God, I'm grateful for all the gifts You've given me, especially the spiritual gift of* _____. *Help me hone that gift, so I can use it for the benefit of Your family.*

If a participant doesn't yet know her spiritual gifts, join her by approaching God in prayer together to ask what her gift(s) might be.

My Next Step

As I come to understand the gift God has given me, I will exercise it in my local congregation by

Keep It in Mind

Every time you're tempted to look longingly at someone else's gift or to elevate your own, remember 1 Corinthians 12:4–5: *"There are different kinds of gifts, but the same Spirit. There are different kinds of service, but the same Lord."*

6

Sĩŋğle-Mĩŋdedŋess
Is a Blessĩŋğ

Acts 21:8–14; 6:2–6; 8:26–35

*I will pour out my Spirit on all people. Your sons
and daughters will prophesy. . . . Even on my
servants, both men and women, I will pour
out my Spirit in those days.*

—Joel 2:28–29

Discovery

Godly parents influence sisters to be dedicated to God.

For Openers

L ikely you, or someone close to you, have spent a season of
adulthood as a single. The percentages of singles in the
population is larger than it's ever been.

My friend Susie, for example, is a single parent, working two jobs
to support herself and her teenage son. She struggles to stay awake
in her few off hours to be available to her son—and to pursue her

calling as a faith-based writer. Like Susie, most singles face time pressures, financial challenges, ministry desires, and a deep need to feel connected to God's family. Yet, singleness also holds special opportunities to wholeheartedly serve Christ, as the apostle Paul (himself a single) explains in 1 Corinthians 7. Susie is experiencing these as she sees poems she's written out of her struggles minister to her friends and their friends.

Today we'll meet four single sisters in Acts 21. We know them by reputation and by their association with their father, apparently a single parent, who sets a powerful example of godliness. In their lives, we'll see the potential for women—single and married—to become all God created us to be.

Getting to Know Them

In Luke's chronicles of the early church, Peter and Paul are main characters. But the supporting cast is vast. One of the most notable among this second tier is Philip the evangelist.

Known to the early church as a man full of the Holy Spirit and wisdom, Philip is among the first deacons selected to handle day-to-day issues in the Jerusalem church. When Christians are scattered by persecution, Philip leads a revival in Samaria, evangelizes along the coast, and settles in Caesarea, a seaport not far from Jerusalem. His availability to Christ is evident as the Spirit directs him into the desert to approach a chariot and help an inquisitive royal official come to faith.

At some point four daughters are born to Philip. These girls are special. They remain virgins and live in their father's home—

perhaps the meeting place of the growing Caesarean church. As they watch Philip's example and experience the influence of Paul (who makes Caesarea his home between missionary journeys), the sisters come to faith in Christ. Perhaps they are Paul's models for his classic statement on singlehood: "An unmarried woman or virgin is concerned about the Lord's affairs: Her aim is to be devoted to the Lord in both body and spirit" (1 Corinthians 7:34).

All four exercise the spiritual gift of prophecy they've received from God. They and their father host Paul and his entourage (including Luke) in their home late in Paul's ministry. The sisters are among those who prophesy about Paul's upcoming persecution. Days later, Paul's arrest unfolds in Jerusalem, as the prophecies of the daughters and others predicted.

The Word Speaks

Imagine yourself a member of a first-century house church as you listen to someone read **Acts 21:8-14**.

To understand the description of Philip as "one of the seven," read **Acts 6:2-6**. What circumstance prompts the calling out of seven deacons? Why did the apostles pray over them? What characteristics equip Philip to be among this elite group? How do these traits make him a great example to his daughters?

The four sisters are among a select few women in the Bible called God's prophetesses. (Others are Miriam, Deborah, Huldah, and

Anna.) Why might God have chosen these sisters to minister to Paul at this moment? What could they offer him?

What Others Say

[Perhaps] they prophesied of Paul's troubles at Jerusalem, as others had done, and dissuaded him from going; or perhaps they prophesied for his comfort and encouragement . . . Here was a further accomplishment of that prophecy, Joel 2:28, of such a plentiful pouring out of the Spirit upon all flesh that their sons and their daughters should prophesy.

—Matthew Henry

Read the quote from Matthew Henry. Presumably, when Luke writes, "we and the people there pleaded with Paul" (v. 12), the prophetesses are among that group. Describe the range of emotions they might be experiencing—as they prophesy and plead with their friend. How is the ministry of these women a fulfillment of Joel's ancient prophecy?

Now read Ajith Fernando's comments. Drawing on Fernando's insights, describe how the ministry of these sisters is an indication of how God's values are opposite to those of this world. How does this scene demonstrate His special gifting of women for His work?

Did You Know?

In that culture unmarried women normally did not have high standing. This may be Luke's way of pointing out that low-status people were included in positions of prominence in the church. . . . Papias, bishop of Hierapolis, said that these daughters were sources of valuable information of what happened in the early years of Christianity. Philip and his daughters may have been one of Luke's information sources.

—Ajith Fernando

Consider Luke's words: "I myself have carefully investigated everything from the beginning" (Luke 1:3a). How might Philip and his daughters have been helpful in this research?

Let's examine a few scenes they experienced firsthand that might have influenced Luke's historical account: Imagine the young women standing in the shadows, watching their father's associate, Stephen, be stoned (Acts 7:54–56, 59–60). Imagine Stephen's otherworldly glow and his last words indelibly etched in their memories. How might they describe this to Luke?

Stephen's stoning scatters the Jerusalem church, including Philip's household. But that doesn't squelch Philip's faith or buy his silence. Discuss what he does instead. (See Acts 8:5–8.) How might this influence his daughters? What might they tell Luke about this era in their lives?

Now read **Acts 8:26-35**. Why might the Spirit have selected Philip? What does this show you about God's value of the Ethiopian man? What might it teach Philip's daughters?

Where We Come In

Bible Background

Philip may have been a widower whose daughters presided over his home and cared for his needs. The text does not indicate the ages of the unnamed women, though their spiritual gifts would suggest a maturity of years and wealth of experience. At least for a time the women were unmarried . . . possibly because of their sense of being especially devoted to God in using their special gift.

—*Women's Study Bible*

Read the Bible Background quote. How does this equip you to encourage a single parent you know (or yourself)? Why did the children in this one-parent household turn out godly and useful to God? How can you apply Philip's example to your household?

Discuss what it means to be "especially devoted to God." What gifts has God given you that He wants you to devote to Him? How will you do that?

Consider Paul's words about single adults in 1 Corinthians 7:32–40. If you are single, how have you seen them play out? If you are married, what can you learn from your single friends? How can you encourage them? How does this passage hearten you? challenge you?

The authors of *Every Woman in the Bible* refer to Philip's daughters as "second-generation Christians . . . following in their father's footsteps." How is this true? How does the statement "God doesn't have grandchildren" apply? What commitment did each of the sisters need to make for herself? Why?

SINGLE-MINDEDNESS IS A BLESSING

Read the story of Joy Scarlatta's family heritage. What decisions did she make for herself? How did her father's example help lead her choices? How did she, in turn, model godliness? How do you intentionally and regularly model godliness?

How It Works Today

When Joy Scarlatta was born, her father, Tony, felt impressed that the Lord was going to use her powerfully. A bi-vocational pastor who preached and tended his spiritual flock, Tony worked as a tailor six days a week. In his shop he kept the local Christian radio station tuned in, drinking in God's Word as he worked. As she tended the register, Joy, too, drank in God's Word—coming to personal faith as a small child. At home, she kept that station on, listening to its music and playing along on her piano.

Later she became a church organist, traveled with a singing group where she often gave salvation messages, and was pianist for Bible studies and conferences. Joy's music partially fulfilled God's promise to her father. But it didn't stop there. She modeled godliness and a high view of God's Word to her daughter. I know, because Joy's married name is Ieron. Through the doors God opens for me to share His Word, my mom's and grandfather's ministries continue.

How did you come to faith in Christ? Whose example did you follow? What drew you? How has your family heritage helped you recognize your need for Christ and the value of serving Him? How has it hindered you? What helps you get past the hindrances?

When did you realize you couldn't entrust your eternal future to someone else's decision for Christ? What did you do as a result?

Note Paul's words in Titus 2:3–5. What lessons about the faith have you learned from older women? What lessons might you be able to share with those who are younger in the faith?

Responding Through Prayer

Spend time praying for each other. If there is a single woman in your group, pray first for her—that God would help her find His purpose in choosing this season of life for her. Continue to pray around your circle, carrying to God each other's needs for fulfillment, fruitfulness, and a reputation of faithfulness in a faithless world.

My Next Step

This week I will

- Seek out a woman who is further along in the faith to be my example.

- Try to live a godly life that younger believers might be able to follow my example.

-

Keep It in Mind

As you process all God is prompting you to do, remember this counsel: *"Live wisely among those who are not Christians, and make the most of every opportunity" (Colossians 4:5 NLT).*

7

The Value of A United Front

Philippians 4:2–9; Hebrews 12:14–15; Matthew 5:21–24

[Jesus prayed,] "May they be brought to complete unity to let the world know that you sent me and have loved them even as you have loved me."

—John 17:23

Discovery

Sisters in conflict wreak havoc on the family.

For Openers

W hy can't you two get along?" the mother half-screams, half-cries at her two feuding daughters. It doesn't matter what sparked this turf battle; it is one among hundreds. The sisters have fought over toys or boys, makeup or chores, friends or privacy. The mother throws up her hands, leaving the girls to fight to the finish.

Before we too quickly chalk up this sibling war to immaturity or adolescent hormones, we might want to examine our own relationships—especially those among women in our families, our workplaces, and our churches—because what we learn as children, we take into adulthood. Feuding denominations and church splits; squabbles that fester and infect those outside the original disagreement; finger pointing that grips households in icy silence—isn't that what the world sees when it looks at us?

Our getting along and presenting a united front to a watching world was so important to Christ that He made it a matter of intense prayer. Perhaps we, and the two otherwise godly women we'll meet today, were on Jesus' mind as He pled, "Make them one, Father," and "Forgive them; they don't know what they do."

Getting to Know Them

Euodia and Syntyche. Mention these two odd-sounding names, and one image comes to mind: a family feud in the body of believers. These are two women whom the apostle Paul chides by name in his otherwise loving letter to the Philippian church.

But let's back up. It isn't all bad for these women. The Bible doesn't give much detail, but we know more than we might think about them. First, they are true, fellow believers. At some moment both spiritual sisters come to a saving knowledge of Jesus Christ. Each confesses her sin. Each accepts the forgiveness He offers. Each commits to obey Him and do life as part of His family. Each probably has prayed, "Forgive us our trespasses, as we forgive those who trespass against us."

Commentators believe the two are deaconesses in the Philippian house church—possibly holding services in their homes. Paul says they are fellow contenders for the gospel, hard workers whose ministry efforts are resulting in much fruit. Not only do the women do ministry with Paul, but they had been working side by side, pulling in the same direction. *Had been*, because now they are pulling in opposite directions—potentially tearing the body apart.

We don't know the cause of their disagreement. It's just as well; because human nature being what it is, we might be tempted to take sides and continue the feud. What we do know is things have gotten bad enough that Paul hears about it from his prison cell in Rome, and he calls on an unnamed fellow worker to help the two reconcile—literally to get them to "agree with each other." Getting two women to agree may be tricky, but it will be worthwhile for oh-so-many reasons.

The Word Speaks

Have someone read aloud **Philippians 4:2-9**, paying special attention to the context around Paul's exhortation and how the body of Christ is to come alongside to encourage reconciliation.

Prayerfully, Focusing on the Good

How have the two women deviated from the ideal example Christ would have them set? Why is this such a big deal?

Christ wants Unity

Bible Background

Usually, athletes competed one against another; in 1:27 Paul asks the church at Philippi to compete together as a team of athletes to help advance the faith that comes through the preaching of the gospel. In the same epistle, he also mentions Euodia and Syntyche as those who were contending for the gospel side by side with himself.

—*The Nelson Study Bible*

Read the Bible Background quote that describes the Greek word we translate as "have contended." Why did the competition change for Euodia and Syntyche from "us against the forces of evil" to "you against me"?

Read the Did You Know? sidebar. How was this dispute bigger than the two participants?

It threatened the entire Congregation

Read **Hebrews 12:14-15**. How could the bitter root of arguing and unforgiveness "cause trouble and defile many"? Why does Paul involve himself and church leadership?

How might the women feel as they hear the letter read to all their fellow believers? How might this feeling alone help facilitate their reconciliation?

Did You Know?

Euodia and Syntyche were involved in the building of the church in Philippi around a.d. 61. Their diligent leadership in the church was recognized by the Apostle Paul himself as well as other believers (Phil. 4:3). Therefore, their dispute threatened to affect the harmony and well-being of the entire congregation.

—*Women's Study Bible*

After exhorting the women, Paul commands them and the church to rejoice, demonstrate gentleness, put away anxiety, be thankful, be prayerful, and live in peace. Comment on the juxtaposition of these and their relevance for the sisters.

Read **Matthew 5:21-24**, where Jesus makes a strong statement about how brothers and sisters in faith ought to behave. How does this reinforce Paul's exhortation?

Jesus has more words about reconciliation in Matthew 18:15–17. How is this consistent with Paul's prescription? How does it differ? Do you think either woman is willing to go to her sister in humility and ask forgiveness before getting Paul's letter? Why or why not?

How would you define *agree?* For example, does it mean both have to exercise the same gifts at the same time? Does it mean neither can have her own thoughts? If not, what does it mean?

Define *unity.* What examples of unity can you think of? Scan John 17. What example of unity does Jesus offer? How does our unity as believers reflect the unity of the Trinity? How is the Godhead united? How does each Member pursue His role while continuing as a united Godhead?

SISTERS IN THE BIBLE

Where We Come In

Read Philippians 2:1–5. List the reasons Paul gives for asking us to be like-minded. Pay special attention to verse 5, where he holds up the ideal example.

What makes us fight each other rather than our real enemy? How can we overcome this? When have you been motivated by the bitter fruits in verses 3–4? What has been the result of acting on these? How many people were affected?

Identify a situation you're experiencing, or have experienced when you disagreed with a fellow believer. Was it a biblical issue or a matter of preference? What did you do about it? How did you (or can you) go about restoring fellowship? Are you willing to take the first step toward reconciliation? Why or why not?

What Others Say

Think about how Jesus identifies with the church. . . . To persecute a brother is to persecute Jesus. To speak roughly of a brother is to speak roughly of Jesus. To touch His disciples is to touch Him.

—*Anne Ortlund*

Read the quote from Anne Ortlund. If her statement is true about Jesus' connection to each believer, how does that affect your desire to argue? How does knowing you're involving Jesus cause you to think and act differently?

68

How It Works Today

Pediatrician Jenny Brown says, "There's a lot of egotism in medicine. I do a lot of work with abused children. [I work together with] law enforcement, social services, district attorneys, defense attorneys, counselors, physicians. There's a delicate balance. You have to learn to not make your own turf the most important thing, or the child suffers.

"In medical school there were people who thought everybody's time was less valuable than theirs, everybody should be their servant. They've been the stars in life, and they expect to continue to be the stars. [But] when you're dealing with hurting kids and hurting parents, nobody cares who's the star. They're looking for a person who is knowledgeable and authoritative, but who's a servant—who cares about them, as well as being able to diagnose their kid's disease. . . . I try to treat my patients like I want to be treated, myself."

Every career path has unique disputes. It says much about our character if we're able to put into practice the wise counsel from Romans 12:18: "As far as it depends on you, live at peace with everyone." Read Dr. Jenny Brown's story about the benefits of this goal in her profession. How would this counsel work in your sphere of influence?

Read the quote from *Praying Like Jesus.* Discuss opinions secular people may hold about Christ-followers. How might our squabbling and unwillingness to forgive brothers and sisters keep seekers from Christ's family?

What Others Say

Is it one message that the world hears when we speak? Is it one heart of love for each other that the world sees when we interact among ourselves? . . . The sad answer to these is that if the world is to judge from the image we most often project, unity would not often be the first descriptor they would choose.

—Julie-Allyson Ieron,
Praying Like Jesus

What squabbles do you know of among churches today? Which battles are really worth fighting? Which should be handled as Paul encouraged the two Philippian women?

What changes can you make immediately that will help those watching you see the value of being a sister of Jesus Christ?

Responding Through Prayer

Make your prayer time silent and personal today. Listen carefully for God's prompting about reconciliation that needs to happen in your life. Then ask Him for the spirit of forgiveness you need to reconcile with your sister or brother—and ask Him to provide the joy and peace He promised would come as a result.

My Next Step

Based on God's prompting, I will be reconciled with _____.

I will begin the process by

Keep It in Mind

This week: *"Be completely humble and gentle; be patient, bearing with one another in love. Make every effort to keep the unity of the Spirit through the bond of peace" (Ephesians 4:2–3).*

8

The Best Sisterhood Of All

Matthew 12:46–50; 6:28–33; Romans 12:9–18

Pointing to his disciples, he said, "Here are my mother and my brothers. For whoever does the will of my Father in heaven is my brother and sister and mother."

—Matthew 12:49–50

Discovery

Jesus offers ultimate sisterhood.

For Openers

In the church my family attended throughout my childhood, we called each other "brother" or "sister." For example, to everyone outside our immediate family, my grandmothers were "Sister Helen" and "Sister Cherubina."

This was especially poignant for Nannie Cherubina. When she came to faith in Christ as a twenty-something mom (shortly after her husband Nick accepted Christ), she did so at the cost of most of her blood-family ties. Born in a strictly religious home, Cherubina converted to Protestantism against the wishes of her family. They refused to associate with her. But her newfound faith community became a complete family that shared more in common with her than a bloodline.

That's the way God planned for the church to operate—as a tight-knit family. Today we'll examine the passage where Jesus calls us His sisters. Imagine—sisters with Christ and sisters with each other—a miraculous birth into a vast family that extends into eternity. All this comes with only one stipulation, though.

Getting to Know Them

By this stage of His public ministry, Jesus is regularly stepping on preconceived notions and traditions. He's offending the powerful by exposing their selfish territorialism and impure motives—making them laughingstocks among the hoi polloi.

A troubling report of these events reaches Jesus' mother and brothers. Perhaps they fear for His life. Certainly they question His sanity. So they come, stand outside where He's teaching, and send a message that they'd like a word with Him privately. There are a few things they'd like to straighten out about His agenda.

Instead of responding, Jesus surveys His inner circle. He sees Peter and the other eleven men who are giving up careers, time with their families, and comforts of home to follow Him. He sees Mary Magdalene, Joanna, and Susanna, three of many wealthy women who travel with His entourage and give their personal finances to bankroll the costs of ministry. Perhaps He looks ahead in time, as only God can, and sees sorrowing women at the foot of His cross and those carrying spices to His tomb to anoint His limp body for burial. Maybe, just maybe, He looks further ahead to see the face of church-worker Phoebe (Romans 16) or Bible-teacher Priscilla (Acts 18) or *you*—pouring over your open Bible today.

Then He speaks astonishing words that say, in essence, "It's not my earthly siblings who have unique claims of kinship with Me; instead it's these men and women who obey my Father's will— only they have the eternal right to be called my brothers and sisters." And so He elevates us to privileges beyond anything we could have expected. For, "to all who received him . . . he gave the right to become children of God" (John 1:12).

The Word Speaks

First, look at Jesus' declaration in **Matthew 12:46-50**. Read the verses aloud, in unison.

What do the men and women following Him every day have to offer Jesus that His brothers and sisters choose not to (at this moment)? What comfort does He find in the company of these faithful friends?

What are some ways Mary and Martha of Bethany, Mary Magdalene, and other sisters meet Jesus' needs? (See Luke 8:2–3 and John 12:1–8.) What motivates them to offer these gifts? What does it cost them to serve Him? Why don't they seem to take any notice of the cost?

Did You Know?

According to W. E. Vine, the Greek word adelphe, translated as sister, not only marks those with a "natural relationship," but also those with a "spiritual kinship with Christ, an affinity marked by the fulfillment of the will of the Father." It is a "spiritual relationship based upon faith in Christ."

Read the Did You Know? sidebar. How is the affinity between spiritual sisters sweeter and more durable than the connection between blood sisters who do not share the same faith?

Turn to Matthew 8:26, and read the quote from the *KJV Bible Commentary.* What's the difference between exhibiting faith that sometimes wavers and intentionally disobeying God? Why doesn't God disown us when our faith sinks low (as Peter's did in Matthew 14:25–31). How does knowing Jesus will confess the faithful before His Father give you additional incentive to remain faithful?

What Others Say

The beauty of this passage can be seen in the fact that while they had left all and followed Him, they were still often "of little faith" (8:26). Yet He was not ashamed to call them brothers (see Heb 2:11).

—*KJV Bible Commentary*

Speculate on what it means to be a sister of Christ. What privileges does it carry? What responsibilities? Read the quote from Matthew Henry. How does Jesus demonstrate His role as our elder Brother? What does it say to you that not only is He asking us to obey, but He willingly obeys the Father's will?

> ## Bible Background
>
> All obedient believers are near akin to Jesus Christ. They wear his name, bear his image, have his nature, are of his family. He loves them, converses freely with them as his relations. He bids them welcome to his table, takes care of them, provides for them, sees that they want nothing that is fit for them, . . . [and] will confess them before men, before the angels, and before his Father.
>
> —Matthew Henry

Comment on each quality Henry lists (e.g., "bear his image," "have his nature," and so forth) and each task our Brother Jesus performs for us.

To discover what Jesus means by doing the will of His Father, read **Matthew 6:28-33**.

What can you learn about God's will in this passage from the Sermon on the Mount? How is worry a way of disobeying God? What specifically might Jesus mean when He directs us to "seek first his kingdom"?

To let the apostle Paul clarify further, read **Romans 12:9-18**. List the evidences of godly love that Paul describes in this passage.

How does sisterly love fit into the Father's will for our lives? How can we exhibit this love? If we all determine to live according to these principles, how will they give evidence to a watching world that we are truly sisters in and of Christ?

Where We Come In

What Others Say

Blest be the tie that binds /
Our hearts in Christian love; /
The fellowship of kindred
minds / Is like to that above.

Before our Father's throne /
We pour our ardent prayers; /
Our fears, our hopes, our aims
are one, / Our comforts and
our cares.

We share our mutual woes, /
Our mutual burdens bear; /
And often for each other flows /
The sympathizing tear.

—John Fawcett

Read the quote from John Fawcett's classic hymn "Blest Be the Tie that Binds." How have you been encouraged by Christian fellowship? When have you needed the support and companionship of sisters and found that need met in your believing friends? What shared understandings did your sisters in Christ have that others might not comprehend?

How does praying for one another contribute to kinship? What kinds of things do you pray for your brothers and sisters in Christ? How are your emotions involved in those prayers?

Name some of the women who have prayed you through tough times. How did God work through them to create ties that bind you with your community of believers?

Examine Jesus' prayer in John 17 for His brothers and sisters. Read verses 20–25, looking for ways to become a partial answer to Jesus' requests. Then look for clues on how to obey God's will for you—which is woven through the fabric of the chapter.

Note the loving way Jesus prays for all who will ever believe (v. 20). How does overhearing that request help you understand how much Jesus values you, individually, as His own sister?

Read the story about the hospital waiting room "sisters." Listen silently for God's prompting about a sister in Christ who needs special care from you just now—perhaps a single parent, someone who is discouraged, a newly widowed woman, or a cancer patient. Do two things right away for the woman God brings to mind: First, pray for her, according to the pattern Jesus sets in John 17; second, come alongside her with tangible help. Share this intent with your group, and pray together about it.

How It Works Today

During my father's six-hour heart bypass surgery a few years ago, I noticed two middle-aged women sitting across the waiting room, flipping through magazines. I recognized them as fellow worshippers from our large congregation.

Were they there for a family member? Sort of, but not exactly. They were there because a fellow member of their single-adult group was having cancer surgery. They'd prayed with her before she went into surgery, and they didn't want her to be alone when she came out.

Eventually, Mom and I received a good word on Dad and were ushered into a family-only waiting area for postoperative critical care. Later, the two women joined us there. Since their friend's prognosis was not good, they stayed several hours to be with her when the doctors gave her the sad news.

Did these women belong in the family-only waiting area? You bet! There is no family like sisters in faith who band together in mutual care—no matter what blood tests may say to the contrary.

Return to the evidences of godly love from Romans 12. Go through that list, and assess how you measure up at each point. Where do you sense God's prompting to take your obedience to the next level? What will you do in response?

Responding Through Prayer

Speak aloud with your sisters in Christ the words of the Lord's Prayer. Let the kinship of shared prayer linger after the amen. If you feel comfortable doing it, share a hug with at least one study friend.

My Next Step

I will follow up this study by

- Praying for and providing help to the sister God placed on my heart.

- Remembering in prayer the needs expressed by those in my group and supporting and encouraging them.

Keep It in Mind

Each morning this week, picture the day when Jesus will present you to His Father with these words: *"Here am I, and the children God has given me" (Hebrews 2:13b).*